50 FAVORITE SONGS FOR KIDS

A POCKETFUL OF PRAISE

COMPILED BY KEN BIBLE

Selected from SING A SONG OF SCRIPTURE

Lillenas Publishing Co.

KANSAS CITY, MO. 64141

Seek Ye First

(Matt. 6:33)

KAREN LAFFERTY

K. L

Seek ye _____ first the _____ king - dom of God

And His _____ righ - teous - ness; _____

And all these things shall be add - ed un - to you.

Hal - le - lu, hal - le - lu - jah.

*Come into His Presence Medley

Arr. by Lyndell Leatherman

COME INTO HIS PRESENCE: unison v. 1; 4-pt. round on v. 4. I WILL ENTER HIS GATES: once.

Come into His Presence
(Round)
(Ps. 100:2; Rom. 10:9; Rev. 5:12)

Unknown   Unknown

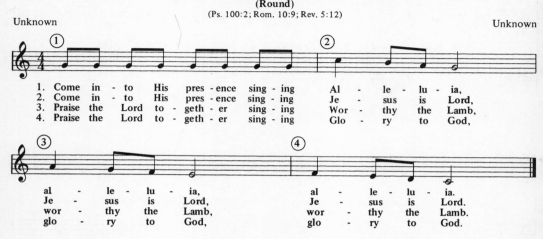

1. Come in - to His pres - ence sing - ing Al - le - lu - ia,
2. Come in - to His pres - ence sing - ing Je - sus is Lord,
3. Praise the Lord to - geth - er sing - ing Wor - thy the Lamb,
4. Praise the Lord to - geth - er sing - ing Glo - ry to God,

al - le - lu - ia,   al - le - lu - ia.
Je - sus is Lord,   Je - sus is Lord.
wor - thy the Lamb,   wor - thy the Lamb.
glo - ry to God,   glo - ry to God.

I Will Enter His Gates
(Ps. 100:4; 118:24)

Adapted   Unknown

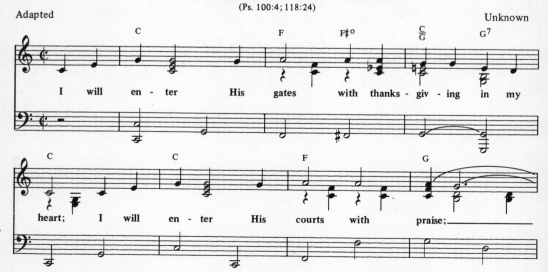

I will en - ter His gates with thanks - giv - ing in my

heart; I will en - ter His courts with praise;

Emmanuel Medley

Arr. by Lyndell Leatherman

JESUS, NAME ABOVE ALL NAMES: twice. EMMANUEL: twice.

Jesus, Name Above All Names

(Matt. 1:21-23; Phil. 2:9-11)

N. H.

NAIDA HEARN

Je - sus, name a - bove all names, beau - ti - ful Sav - ior, glo - ri - ous Lord;_____ Em - man - u - el, God__ is with us, bless - ed Re - deem - er, liv - ing Word.

Emmanuel

(Matt. 1:23)

B. McG.

BOB McGEE

Servant Medley

Arr. by Lyndell Leatherman

SERVANT OF ALL: once. MAKE ME A SERVANT: twice.

Servant of All

(Mark 10:43-44)

M. R.

MICHAEL RYAN

Make Me a Servant

(Mark 10:43-44)

K. W.

KELLY WILLARD

Soon and Very Soon

(Rev. 21:1-4)

A. C.

ANDRAÉ CROUCH

*Verses 1 & 2 on recording/trax.

jah, hal - le - lu - jah, hal - le - lu - jah!

The Trees of the Field

(Is. 55:12)

STEFFI GEISER RUBIN

STUART DAUERMANN

You shall go out with joy___ and be led

forth with peace.___ The moun - tains and the

hills will break forth be - fore you; There'll be

shouts of joy,___ and all the trees of the

Love and Praise Medley

Arr. by Lyndell Leatherman

I LOVE YOU, LORD: once. I WILL OFFER YOU PRAISE: vv. 1 & 3. I WILL BLESS THE LORD: once.

I Love You, Lord

(Ps. 116:1-2; 145:1-2)

L. K.

LAURIE KLEIN

I Will Offer You Praise

(Ps. 34:1; 63:5-7; 71:8; 1 Thess. 5:18)

G. J.

GARY JOHNSON

I will of - fer You praise/thanks — when the sun meets the dew, And I will
(love)

of - fer You praise/thanks at the noon's bright-est hue. I will
(love)

of - fer You praise/thanks — when the star-light is due; And if I wake in the
(love)

night, Lord, I'll still be prais - ing/thank - ing You. You.
(lov - ing)

I Will Bless the Lord

(Ps. 145:1-2, 8-9, 17)

F. H.

FRANK HERNANDEZ

This Is the Day Medley

Arr. by Lyndell Leatherman

SING AND CELEBRATE: twice. THIS IS THE DAY: twice.

Sing And Celebrate

(Ps. 118:24)

C. F. B.

CHARLES F. BROWN

This Is the Day

(Ps. 118:24)

L. G.

LES GARRETT

King of Kings Medley

Arr. by Lyndell Leatherman

WE WILL GLORIFY: vv. 1, 2, 3, 4 (take 3rd ending). KING OF KINGS: once.

We Will Glorify

(Ex. 3:14; Rev. 4:8-11; 5:8-14; 17:14)

TWILA PARIS

1. We will glo - ri - fy the King of Kings; We will glo - ri - fy the ___ Lamb;
(2. Lord Je -) ho - vah reigns in maj - es - ty, We will bow be - fore His ___ throne;

We will glo - ri - fy the Lord of Lords, Who ___ is the great I Am. 2. Lord Je-
We will wor - ship Him in right-teous-ness; We will wor - ship Him a -

lone. 3. He is Lord of heav - en, Lord of earth; He is
lu - jah to the King of Kings, Hal - le -
glo - ri - fy the King of Kings, We will

King of Kings

(Is. 9:6; Rev. 19:16)

SOPHIE CONTY and
NAOMI BATYA

Ancient Hebrew Folksong

He's Everything to Me

(Ps. 19:1; 145:18; Matt. 1:21; John 4:42)

R. C.

RALPH CARMICHAEL

1. In the stars His hand-i - work I see, On the wind He speaks with maj - es - ty. Though He rul - eth o - ver land and sea, What is that to me? What is that to me?

2. I will cel - e - brate na - tiv - i - ty, For it has a place in his - to - ry. Sure, He came to set His peo - ple free;

Till by faith I met Him face to face, And I felt the won-der

How Excellent Your Name

(Ps. 8)

P. J.

PETER JACOBS

O Lord, our Lord, how ex - cel-lent Your name is, how ex - cel-lent Your name in all the earth. Your glo - ry fills the heav - ens be - yond the far - thest star; How ex - cel-lent Your name in all the earth.

When I think a-bout the heav -ens, the moon and all the stars,

I won- der what You ev - er saw in me.

But You took me and You loved me, and You've giv- en me a crown;

and now I'll praise Your name e - ter - nal-

ly.

D.C. al Fine

*Bible Medley

Arr. by Lyndell Leatherman

THY WORD HAVE I HID IN MY HEART: once. INPUT/OUTPUT: once, both vv.

Thy Word Have I Hid in My Heart

(Ps. 119:11)

Adapted

Unknown

Input/Output (The Computer Song)

(Ps. 119:11; Phil. 2:5; Col. 3:1-2)

KATHIE HILL and
GARY McSPADDEN

K. H.

In - put, out - put—what goes in is what comes out. In - put, out - put— that is what it's all a - bout.

In - put, out - put—your mind is a com-put-er whose In - put, out - put dai - ly you must

choose. 1. Let the Bi - ble be your pri - ma - ry feed; It's got all the
2. If your print-out reads___ to lie or cheat, There's some da - ta

da - ta you need.___ Talk to Je - sus all the time; That's the way that
you should de-lete. De - bug your mind of sin - ful bytes; Then___ you will

you can stay on line! In - put, out - put—
op - er - ate all right!

His Love Medley

Arr. by Lyndell Leatherman

NOBODY CARED: all vv. OH, HOW HE LOVES YOU AND ME: both vv.

Nobody Cared

(Matt. 4:1-2; 21:1-11; 27:22-44; Luke 2:1-7; John 6:5-15, 26)

JACK HAYFORD

J. H.

1. No - bod - y want - ed Him;
2. No - bod - y laud - ed Him;
(D.S.) No - bod - y want - ed Him;

no - bod - y cared. No - bod - y want - ed Him;
no - bod - y sang. No crowd ap - plaud - ed Him;
no one re - mained. They on - ly taunt - ed Him

no_____ one_____ shared In the prom - ise He brought as a
no_____ bells_____ rang When He went to the des - ert to
when His cross was stained With the blood free - ly giv'n for a

Oh, How He Loves You and Me

(John 15:13; 1 John 4:9-10)

K. K.

KURT KAISER

1. Oh how He loves you and me; Oh, how He loves you and me. He gave His life—what more could He give? Oh, how He loves you; oh, how He loves me; Oh, how He loves you and me.

2. Je - sus to Cal - v'ry did go, His love for sin - ners to show. What He did there brought hope from de - spair.

*I Will Sing Medley

Arr. by Lyndell Leatherman

I WILL SING OF THE MERCIES: once. I WILL CALL UPON THE LORD: once, with repeats.

I Will Sing of the Mercies

(Ps. 89:1)

Adapted from Psalm 89:1

Unknown

I Will Call upon the Lord

(2 Sam. 22:47; Ps. 18:3)

Adapted by M. O'S.

MICHAEL O'SHIELDS

It's a Miracle

(Ps. 104; 139)

W. J. and GLORIA GAITHER

WILLIAM J. GAITHER

*1. What drives the stars with-out mak-ing a sound?_____
2. Who shows the birds how to make a good nest?_____
*(3.) spring makes a brook and a brook makes a stream, The

Why don't they crash_____ when they're spin-ning a-round?
How can the geese_____ fly so far with-out rest?
stream makes the riv-er wa-ter fresh as can be.

What holds me up_____ when the world's up-side down?)
Why do the ducks_____ go_____ south and not west? } I
Who puts the salt in when it gets to the sea?)

know—_____ it's a mir-a-cle._____ Who tells the
What makes a
(3.) There are thou-sands of

He can make a mir - a - cle of me!　　　　3. When a

Sandy Land
(Matt. 7:24-27)

K. L.　　　　　　　　　　　　　　　　　　KAREN LAFFERTY

Don't build your house on the sand - y land,_____ Don't build it too near the

shore._____ Well, it might look kind of nice, but you'll have to build it twice; Oh, you'll

have to build your house once more.　　　　more.　　　　You bet - ter

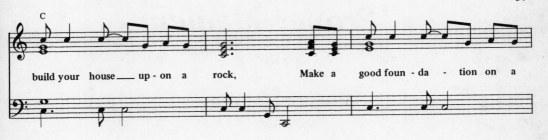

build your house — up - on a rock, Make a good foun - da - tion on a

sol - id spot. — Oh, the storms may come and go, — But the

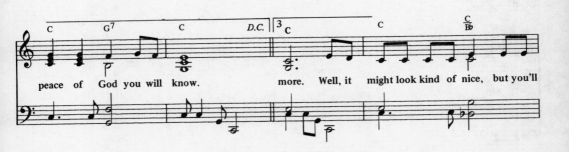

peace of God you will know. more. Well, it might look kind of nice, but you'll

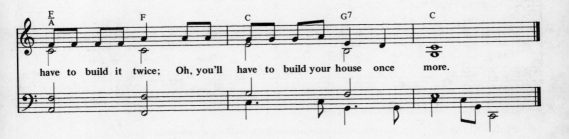

have to build it twice; Oh, you'll have to build your house once more.

*Prayer Medley

Arr. by Lyndell Leatherman

WHISPER A PRAYER: vv. 1 & 2. WHEN WE TALK TO HIM: twice.

Whisper a Prayer

(Ps. 55:16-17; Luke 12:40)

Unknown   Unknown

1. Whis - per a pray'r in the morn - ing,
2. God an - swers pray'r in the morn - ing,
3. Je - sus may come in the morn - ing,

Whis - per a pray'r at noon,_____
God an - swers pray'r at noon,_____
Je - sus may come at noon,_____

Whis - per a pray'r in the eve - ning To
God an - swers pray'r in the eve - ning To
Je - sus may come in the eve - ning So

keep_____ your heart in tune._____
keep_____ your heart in tune._____
keep_____ your heart in tune._____

When We Talk to Him

(Ps. 34:15, 17; 145:18)

DAVID STEELE

D. S.

When we talk to Him_____ He will hear_____ us;_____

_____ He will lis - ten to all that we say._____

For the Lord of all is our clos - est

friend; He is with __ us as now we pray._____

I Wonder How It Felt

(Gen. 6-8; Ex. 2:1-10; 1 Sam. 17; Prov. 3:5-6; Dan. 6; Jon. 1; Acts 16:23-24)

W. J. G. and GLORIA GAITHER

WILLIAM J. GAITHER

*1. I won-der how it felt to wake up in the bel-ly of a
(2. I) won-der how it felt to meet___ big Go-li-ath in the
*(3. I) won-der how it'd be to watch your ba-by broth-er in the
*(4. I) won-der how it felt to spend the night with No-ah in the

whale. I won-der how it felt to
field. I won-der how it felt to
Nile; I won-der who would come, a
zoo; I won-der how it felt to

spend the night with Si-las in the jail.
know the mouths of li-ons have been sealed.
prin-cess or a hun-gry croc-o-dile.
sleep be-side a smell-y kan-ga-roo.

I'm just a child, my life is still be-fore me; I just can't

*Verses 1, 3, 4 on recording/trax.

wait to see what God has for me. But I know that I will trust Him, And I'll

wait to see what life will be for me.

me.

2. I
3. I
4. I

Father I Adore You
(Round)
(Matt. 16:24-25; 22:37-38; 2 Cor. 5:14-15)

TERRYE COELHO

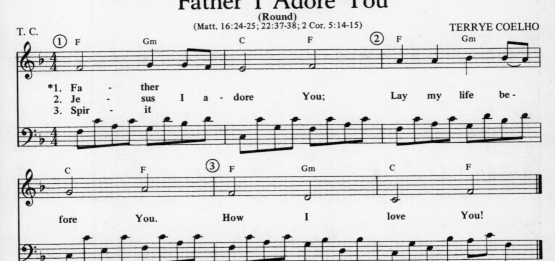

*1. Fa - ther I a - dore You; Lay my life be -
2. Je - sus
3. Spir - it

fore You. How I love You!

We Were Made to Love the Lord

(Gen. 1; Matt. 22:36-38)

K. H. and J. McM.

KATHIE HILL and JANET McMAHAN

*Verses 1 & 3 on recording/trax.

Cares Chorus

(1 Pet. 5:7)

K. W.

KELLY WILLARD

cares up-on You.

No Mountain High Enough

(Rom. 8:35-39)

C. K.

CHARLES KIRBY

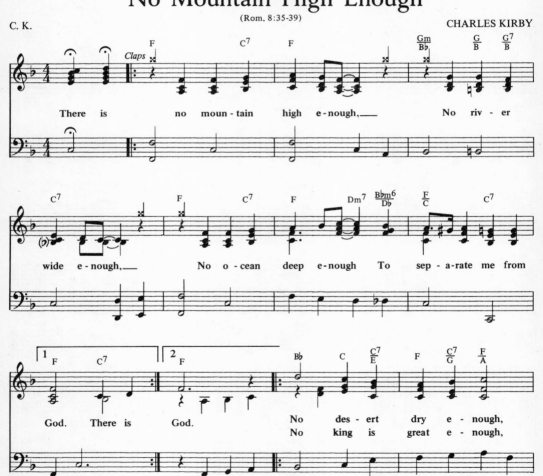

There is no moun-tain high e-nough,___ No riv-er wide e-nough,___ No o-cean deep e-nough To sep-a-rate me from God. There is God.

No des-ert dry e-nough,
No king is great e-nough,

*Invitation Medley

Arr. by Lyndell Leatherman

RIGHT NOW: twice. INTO MY HEART: both vv.

Right Now

(Josh. 24:15)

O. S.

OTIS SKILLINGS

Right now, right now, Com - mit your life right now. De-
cide to live your life for Him right now, right now.

Into My Heart

(Rev. 3:20)

vs. 1–H. D. C.
vs. 2–Unknown

HARRY D. CLARKE

1. In - to my heart, in - to my heart, Come
2. Rule in my heart, rule in my heart, Thou

For God so loved the world
that he gave his one and only Son,
that whoever believes in him shall not perish
but have eternal life (John 3:16, NIV).

Here I am!
I stand at the door and knock.
If anyone hears my voice and opens the door,
I will come in and eat with him,
and he with me (Rev. 3:20, NIV).

*Bless His Name Medley

Arr. by Lyndell Leatherman

BLESS HIS HOLY NAME: once. BLESSED BE THE LORD: once, both vv.

Bless His Holy Name
(Ps. 103:1-2)

A. C.

ANDRAÉ CROUCH

Bless the Lord, O my soul, and all that is with-
in me bless His ho - ly name.
He has done great things, He has done great things,
He has done great things, bless His ho - ly name.

Blessed Be the Lord

(Ps. 28:6-7)

DAVID STEELE

*Trust in the Lord Medley

Arr. by Lyndell Leatherman

TRUST IN THE LORD: twice. TEACH ME, LORD: once.

Trust in the Lord
(Prov. 3:5-6)

Adapted from Prov. 3:5,6

RICK and SYLVIA POWELL

Teach Me, Lord

(1 Sam. 3:10; Ps. 25:4-5)

LINDA REBUCK

TOM FETTKE

Clap Your Hands Medley

Arr. by Lyndell Leatherman

CLAP YOUR HANDS (Jacobs): vv. 1 & 2 with refrain. CLAP YOUR HANDS (Johnson): twice.

Clap Your Hands
(Ps. 47)

P. J.

PETER JACOBS

come, praise His ho-ly name for-ev-er. Come bless the Lord, ev-'ry-

bod-y, with a voice of praise!

Clap Your Hands

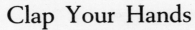

(Ps. 47:1)

GARY JOHNSON

G. J.

(claps)

Clap your hands, shout for joy, sing to

God ev-'ry-one. Clap your hands, shout for

1st time: D.C.
2nd time: Fine

joy, sing to God from sun to sun.

*Call and Answer Medley

Arr. by Lyndell Leatherman

GOD CALLS US: vv. 1 & 3. THIS IS MY PRAYER: once.

God Calls Us

(Matt. 9:36-38; John 20:21)

LINDA REBUCK

TOM FETTKE

This Is My Prayer

(Matt. 16:24; 22:37-38; 2 Cor. 5:14-15)

D. H.

DOUG HOLCK

I want to love You, Lord; I want to

serve You, Lord; I want to please You, Lord;

This is my prayer. This is my prayer.

Love the Lord your God
with all your heart
and with all your soul
and with all your mind.
This is the first and greatest commandment (Matt. 22:37-38, NIV).

*Disciples Medley

Arr. by Lyndell Leatherman

THERE WERE TWELVE DISCIPLES: once. TWELVE IS NOT ENOUGH: vv. 1, 6, 7.

There Were Twelve Disciples

(Matt. 10:1-4)

Anonymous

GEORGE A. MINOR

Twelve Is Not Enough

(Matt. 9:9; 10:1-4; 17:1-8; 26:33-35; 28:16-20; Luke 10:1-2; 24:13-31; John 20:24-29)

T. W.

TED WUERFFEL

*1. Pe - ter said he would not   leave the Mas - ter;   Then he ran a - way in   deep - est fear.
2. James and John were hap-py   on the moun-tain,   When they saw the Lord trans - fig - ured there;
3. Mat-thew was a hat - ed   tax col - lect - or,   Send - ing Jew-ish mon - ey   off to Rome.
4. Cleo-pas and his friend were   bro - ken-heart-ed;   Their Re-deem-er had been   cru - ci - fied.
5. Thom-as doubt-ed that the   Lord has ris - en;   Je - sus came a - gain so   he could see:
*6. Je - sus called the twelve and   then called oth - ers;   Sent them out to wit - ness   two by two.
*7. "Go in - to the world and   preach the Gos-pel!   Bring the news of vic - t'ry   o - ver sin!

Lat - er he be -came a   fam - ous wit - ness,   Preach-ing in the Lord sal - va - tion dear.
But they did not know the   cross would fol - low,   And the bit - ter cup so   hard to share.
Je - sus came and called him,   "Rise and fol - low."   Now his trea-sure is his   heav'n-ly home.
At Em-ma-us Je - sus   broke bread with them;   Sud - den-ly their eyes were   o - pened wide.
"Bless-ed are the ones who   have not seen Me,   Yet who hear the mes - sage   and be - lieve."
Twelve be-came in time a   count - less num-ber;   Saints a-live! and now He's   call - ing you.
Bap -tize in the Name that   chas - es Sa - tan!   Share the love of Je - sus;   bring them in!"

*Verses 1, 6, and 7 on recording trax.

*Worship the Lord Medley

Arr. by Lyndell Leatherman

SING HALLELUJAH (TO THE LORD): vv. 1 & 2. HE IS LORD: once. LORD, WE PRAISE YOU: vv. 1 & 2.

Sing Hallelujah (to the Lord)

(1 Cor. 15:20; Rev. 19:1, 4-6)

LINDA STASSEN

Additional verses

* 2. Jesus is risen from the dead.
3. Christ is the Lord of heav'n and earth.
4. Praise be to God forevermore.
5. Sing hallelujah to the Lord.

He is Lord

(Phil. 2:9-11)

Unknown   Unknown

He is Lord,   He is Lord;   He is ris - en from the

dead and He is Lord!   Ev - 'ry knee shall bow, ev - 'ry

tongue con - fess that Je - sus Christ is Lord.

Lord, We Praise You

(Heb. 13:15)

OTIS SKILLINGS

O. S.

*1. Lord,   we   praise   You.   Lord,   we   praise   You.
*2. Lord,   we   love   You.   Lord,   we   love   You.
3. Al - le - lu - ia!   Al - le - lu - ia!

Lord,   we   praise   You. We   praise   You,   Lord.
Lord,   we   love   You. We   love   You,   Lord.
Al - le - lu - ia!   We   give   You   praise.

Multiply

(John 6:5-13, 51)

D. R. and D. H.

DOTTIE RAMBO and DAVID HUNTSINGER

1. Lit-tle bare-foot boy,_____ run-ning through the sand,
2. Hey there, Chris-tian, trav-'ling through the land,

What-cha got_____ in that bas-ket in your hand? There's five thou-sand peo-ple
What-cha gon-na do with the Word in your hand? There's hun-gry_____ peo-ple

wait-ing to be fed; How'd you like to share_____ your_____ fish and bread?
wait-ing to be fed; Thir-sty for the wa-ter and the Liv-ing Bread.

How'd you like to share_____ your_____ fish and bread? To sum it all up, you
Thir-sty for the wa-ter and the Liv-ing Bread.

sim-ply di-vide; Watch your fish and bread just mul-ti-ply.

*or Group I, followed by Group II.

Philippians 4:13

H. W. G.

HOMER W. GRIMES

TOPICAL INDEX

ALPHABETICAL INDEX